Seasons of Chalk
In the Enchanted Forest

A Second Collection of Chalk Board Stories & Poems

(told at The SkyGarden)

Stories & Illustrations by Jennifer Moore

For Sissy, my perfect, special, lifelong friend

Copyright © 2024 by Jennifer Moore

All rights reserved

No part of this book may be reproduced in any manner whatsoever,
without written permission except in the case of brief quotations
embodied in critical articles and reviews.

First Printing, 2024

ISBN 979-8-218-39545-2

Contents

Root Babies Wake Up

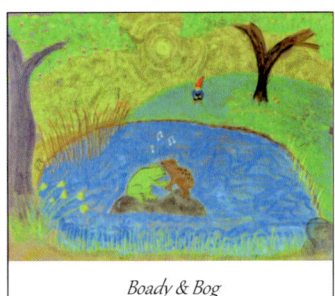
Boady & Bog

Transformation of Wooly Bear

Gold at the End of the Rainbow

Perfect Special Friend

The Most Important Rainbow Fairy

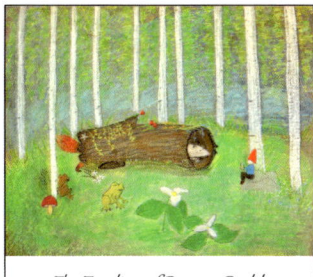
The Tending of Possum Buddy

The Wandering Chick

Water Song

A Lovely Stone for Dragon

Carpenter & Honey Bee

The Pine upon the Hill

Root Babies Wake Up

Once upon a time, in the Enchanted Forest, the sun fairies and the rain fairies danced happily into spring. The rain fairies swirled through the air, plopping fat drops of water onto the earth below, and the sun fairies wove long streams of warm, golden rays that stirred and roused the roots, sleeping deep in the earth. Between the rain and sun fairies, the Enchanted Forest slowly started to wake.

Down deep underground, three little root babies slept soundly all winter long. Now, the drip, drip, drip, of water and the feel of the warm earth slowly woke them from their slumber. Little Rhubarb Root sat up and stretched, "What a wonderful sleep I had!" he said. "Wake up, Rose Root and Raspberry Root! Spring has come!" One by one, the little root babies awoke, and began their journey up, up, up towards the sun. They popped their heads up out of the earth, and saw many of their dear friends of the forest. Beautiful Blue Bird greeted Raspberry Root, "Welcome back, Raspberry Root! I am so happy to see you! How I've missed your delicious raspberries!"

"Happy Spring, Blue Bird! I'll need some time to grow and become strong, but I will have raspberries for you soon!"

Monarch Butterfly fluttered around Rose Root's head, "Hello, flower-friend, I'm back from the southern forests! I can hardly wait to smell your beautiful rose buds and taste your sweet nectar!"

"Welcome home, butterfly! My buds will come soon. When they open, you may drink all the nectar you'd like!"

Possum Buddy, delighted to see Rhubarb Root, said, "I'm glad you're back! Beaver and I always look forward to our evening snack of delicious rhubarb stalks!"

"Well, you won't have to wait much longer! I will grow big and tall this spring. You will soon have plenty of stalks to enjoy!"

Then the root babies set their roots. Again, the wind fairies blew the rain fairies in, and they danced their rain dance. Again, the sun fairies came with warm rays of sunshine. The root babies stretched up, up, up - towards the sun! Raspberry Root grew tall canes that produced the most delicious berries. Rose Root put out long, lovely stems with fat, pale buds that opened into beautiful, red flowers. Rhubarb Root sent up an abundance of pinkish red, and green, stalks - thick and tart, with huge leaves.

The forest bloomed into summer, and the lovely creatures of the forest rejoiced with great jubilation and gratitude for the abundance and beauty that the forest offered.

Boady & Bog

Boady and Bog, the toad and frog, were cousins from the forest.
Both were quite sweet, and had little, webbed feet, and together could sing such a chorus!

When the sky would rain, they'd sing their refrain - each trying to out-sing the other.
Bog would croon out a trill. His throat sac would fill, looking like a balloon, green in color.

Then Boady would start, singing straight from his heart, a croak heard throughout the woods.
Together they'd sing a full-throated ring just as beautifully loud as they could.

One day, Bog, the frog, as he sat on a log, had something he thought he'd suggest,
"Boady, my kin, I think we could win if we entered a singing contest."

So Boady and Bog, the toad and the frog, packed up and left the meadow,
Certain they'd find praise of some kind, sharing their duetted bellow.

The forest grew still, with no ribbit, nor shrill; the woodland, no longer the same.
And all were so glum, missing the hum, as the cousins went off to find fame.

They lost it of course, because Boady went hoarse on the day they were scheduled to sing.
They didn't find fame, and they never became the stars they hoped talent would bring.

Home, they came, with a wee bit of shame, But, what did the cousins find?
The Enchanted Forest was filled with a chorus from voices of every kind!

Birds and bees, flowers and trees - forest fairy and gnome,
Sang out loud, how happy and proud, to have Boady and Bog back home.

And Boady and Bog, the toad and frog, well, they finally understood;
There's naught to be gained seeking fortune and fame, when loved in your own back wood.

The Transformation of Wooly Bear

𝕺𝖓𝖈𝖊 𝖚𝖕𝖔𝖓 𝖆 𝖙𝖎𝖒𝖊, in the Enchanted Forest, a little wooly bear crawled out from under a log. The fuzzy black and brown caterpillar had spent all winter curled into a little ball under the leaves. Now, spring had come to the forest. The rain fairies had soaked the forest floor, and the sun fairies had warmed it with golden rays of sunshine. The plants and creatures of the forest had begun to stir.

Wooly Bear crawled along the ground looking for a young, sturdy, sapling with lots of new leaves. He was very hungry, and a little grumpy. Shortly, he came upon Charlie Gnome, who was scattering bergamot and aster seeds in a little clearing.

"I see that you're awake, my little Wooly Bear! The seeds I spread will soon transform to flowers, everywhere! The bees will be so happy, and the butterflies will swoon. Come and throw some seeds with me - let's see what soon shall bloom!"

But Wooly Bear would have none of Charlie Gnome's happy mood. He groaned, "I'm *still* a caterpillar! I went to bed last winter a caterpillar and I woke up a caterpillar! It seems I'm *never* going to be a butterfly!"

Charlie Gnome stopped scattering seeds and looked at Wooly Bear with great consideration.

"I'm afraid in this, you're right, my friend. You're not a butterfly. But you'll transform to something new, and bravely soar the sky. And when the sun goes down, you'll work into the night. A messenger to all of us; a tiger taking flight!"

"A tiger?! Silly gnome - caterpillars don't turn into tigers!" grumbled Wooly Bear as he scooted off to find a green leaf for breakfast. Charlie Gnome had a twinkle in his eye as he watched the grumpy caterpillar crawl away. He gave a little chuckle and returned to scattering seeds.

Spring continued to transform the forest. The buds on the trees turned to leaves. Charlie Gnome's little seeds had also transformed into lovely plants with fat little buds that would soon open into beautiful flowers. Wooly Bear, who had filled his tummy with lots of green leaves, had gone back to bed in a cocoon he had made for himself.

One late spring evening, as the sun was going down, Wooly Bear broke out of his cocoon. It had finally happened! He was no longer a caterpillar! He had transformed, just as Charlie Gnome had told him that he would! It was true – he was *not* a butterfly. And though he wasn't *exactly* a mighty jungle tiger, Wooly Bear had transformed into a lovely tiger moth, with orange tiger stripes and yellow leopard spots! The lovely moth flew bravely into the dark, stopping briefly to drink the nectar from the flowers that Charlie Gnome had planted, before continuing into the night sky to begin his important work of delivering messages.

Gold at the End of the Rainbow

Once upon a time, in the Enchanted Forest, a wee, green leprechaun was hard at work. He was busy making a pair of tiny pink slippers. The slippers were to be a gift from the rainbow fairies to their dear mother. The leprechaun was very talented in making little shoes for all of the fairies and gnomes that lived in the forest. He would make their tiny shoes, and they would pay him a gold coin. He kept all of his gold coins in a little, black pot that he hid inside an old hollow tree, next to his shoe-making tool kit. After he had finished making the beautiful, pink slippers for the rainbow fairies' mother, blue rainbow fairy came to pay him his gold coin.

"Such a lovely pair of slippers!" blue rainbow fairy crooned! "Mother will be delighted!" and the fairy gathered up the slippers and flew off.

The leprechaun took his new, gold coin and hurried away to hide it in the tree. At that very moment however, the little, green dragon, who lived in a cave, in Purple Mountain, was flying high above, in the clouds. As the leprechaun went to place his shiny coin into his pot, the gold reflected the light of the sun, creating a dazzling flash that caught the eye of the dragon. The dragon simply could not help himself, for he loved *all* shiny things! He swept down on the pot of gold, and flew it off to his cave.

Several days later, when the leprechaun returned to the tree to retrieve materials for a pair of fairy slippers, he was greatly dismayed to find that his gold was gone!

Now, all those that live in the forest know how much the little green dragon loves gold and all things that sparkle. So, when news of the leprechaun's missing pot of gold reached Charlie Gnome, he knew exactly what had happened, and headed off to Purple Mountain. Charlie tip-toed quietly past the sleeping dragon to the very back of the cave, where he found the leprechaun's little, black pot of gold among many other piles of shiny jewels, crystals, and scattered gold and silver. He gathered up the pot and returned it to the leprechaun, who was very happy to get it back. Then Charlie Gnome summoned his friend, Tiger Moth, the night messenger, and sent a message to the rainbow fairies.

The next day, the rainbow fairies came to the leprechaun and offered to keep his pot of gold safe at the end of their rainbow; for the rainbow always appeared in a different place. The leprechaun happily agreed.

~ And the pot of gold was never stolen again!

Perfect Special Friend

Once upon a time, a little boy swung in a mulberry tree just outside the Enchanted Forest. Birds pecked happily at mulberries hanging from branches. Bees in the meadow, made sleepy, warm, buzzing sounds as they flew from flower to flower. The clear blue sky was alive with darting dragonflies and beautifully colored butterflies, twirling and dancing in the air. Everything appeared to be happy and bright – *except* for the little boy, dangling his feet from the swing. He was actually a bit glum, because his older sister was off playing with friends her own age, and had left him all alone. "I wish I had a special friend who loved me, and who I could play with every day," he whispered sadly. As he continued to swing, feeling very sorry for himself, he spied a squirrel with a yellow tail. He'd never seen such a thing! He hopped from his swing, and ran toward the little squirrel, who was suddenly startled by the quick movement of the boy. The squirrel darted back into the Enchanted Forest.

The boy followed the squirrel, who jumped a creek and continued on into the trees. He stepped carefully across several stones in the water, following the path of the squirrel. He could no longer see the squirrel, but a little red fox hopped about under a tree, croaking, "Ribbit! Ribbit! I'm a frog!" The boy, fascinated at a fox acting like a frog, stopped to watch. He laughed at the funny little fox. When she heard him, she froze like a deer – staring at him for several seconds. Suddenly, no longer a frog, the little fox, (who had a bushy tail, red ears, black eyes and a nose, but was *always* just whatever Dew Drop chose), became a beautiful deer - gracefully leaping over the bushes and bounding quickly out of sight. He tried to follow her, but only ended up even deeper into the forest. For a long while, the boy wandered around, amazed at the sights and sounds of the forest. Soon, however, he realized that he really had no idea how to get back to the village. The forest grew still, and darkness began to settle. The boy, now quite frightened, sat under a pine tree and pulled his knees up close to his body. "If I had a special friend, we would hold hands and find our way out of the forest together," he cried. The tall pine tree, moved by the boy's tears, lowered its branches and wrapped the boy in soft, warm, pine boughs, and the little boy slept. In the morning, a soft wind blew through the branches of the tree. They fell away from the boy as he awoke. The tree had made him feel so safe during the night. The boy spoke kind words to the pine tree, thanking it for holding him while he slept. Looking into the forest, the boy wondered what he would do next. He wished the lovely pine could go with him. Suddenly, a wind fairy tousled the little boy's curls and gently took up his hand.

"Come, little friend," whispered the wind fairy. Hand in hand, the boy and wind fairy weaved in and out of the trees, rustling through the branches and leaving swirls of leaves and dandelion fluff behind them. After some time, the fairy landed at the foot of a big purple mountain and sat the little boy down on a large rock, then quietly blew away.

"How wonderful to fly with a fairy! I hope the wind fairy returns soon." But as soon as the boy had this thought, a funny, little helper-gnome popped his head out from behind a tree. "I see you there, you seem quite lost - sitting on that rock. Come and take my hand, dear boy. It's time that we should walk." Charlie Gnome gave a little chuckle, then approaching the boy, gently took his hand and led him all the way to the creek. As they walked, the little boy laughed at the gnome's silly rhymes and jokes. Suddenly, the gnome stopped and pointed, "Look! A squirrel whose tail is yellow! Let's see if she might help a fellow!"

The boy looked to where the gnome was pointing and saw the little yellow-tailed squirrel happily eating a crab apple. Instead of running away, however, the squirrel bounced over to the boy. She folded his hand around her perfectly beautiful, bright, yellow tail, and with a click, click of her tongue, she led the little boy away. He turned back to bid his new friend to follow, but the gnome was already gone. The squirrel led the boy back across the creek and to the edge of the meadow. There, they heard voices. The squirrel pulled her tail from the boy's hand, and silently disappeared back into the forest. The boy was just about to call out to the squirrel, when he saw a search party of people from his village approaching the forest. Leading the group was the little boy's sister. When she saw his bright, yellow, floppy curls, she cried tears of joy, and ran quickly to take up his warm, little hand in hers. Together, they walked home to the village. There was great rejoicing at the return of the little boy, who realized that he had *always* had that perfect, special friend - at just the right time – at just the right place.

The Most Important Rainbow Fairy

𝒪nce upon a time, in the Enchanted Forest, six, wee, rainbow fairies floated lazily on lily pads. The Sun shone brightly, without a cloud in the sky, and dragonflies skimmed across the water leaving lovely, silvery ripples. Blue rainbow fairy dipped tiny toes into the water and mused, "I wonder when it will rain next."

"Oh, not until the rain fairies decide to come," said red rainbow fairy. "The rain fairies are the *most* important creatures of the forest, you know."

"Well, not as important as the helper-gnomes," said yellow rainbow fairy. "They help *all* of the forest creatures."

"Yes, of course they do," replied orange rainbow fairy, (who was very clever), "however, without bees and butterflies, there would *be* no forest, for there would be no pollination of flowers and trees. *They* are certainly the most important creatures of the forest"

Green rainbow fairy's head popped up, "Well, I happen to know that yellow-tailed squirrel has helped to plant many of the trees in the forest too! – Like acorn trees and walnut trees and hickory! So, she's very important as well."

"Acorn trees are really actually *oak* trees," corrected the very clever orange rainbow fairy. Then purple rainbow fairy chimed in, "Yes, trees and flowers are certainly important, but personally, the beautiful music of the forest is very lovely, and it's one of my favorite things. That wonderful music wouldn't exist without Bog Frog, Boady Toad, the cicadas, and the song birds. These are *clearly* the most important creatures of the forest."

The rainbow fairies went on like this for quite some time, arguing back and forth about whose job was the most important in the forest and why. Father Sun watched from the sky. He was happy that the little fairies realized all of the work that went into making the forest the wonderful place that it was, but, was also a bit concerned that the rainbow fairies were arguing about whose job was *most* important. "Silly, little fairies!" he thought, and he pulled the prism from the sky. Suddenly all of the rainbow fairies went gray. They sat up from their lily pads, quite startled, and immediately stopped arguing.

"If you can tell me the most important color of the rainbow, I will return your colors," said Father Sun.

The little rainbow fairies looked at each other with great dismay. No longer were they bright and colorful. Instead, they looked bleak and drab. Then one gray rainbow fairy whispered quietly, "But... how can one of us be the most important? We can't make a rainbow unless we're *all* of the colors."

"Yes," agreed another gray rainbow fairy sadly, "we *all* have to be there to make the perfect rainbow."
The other rainbow fairies nodded in agreement.

Then Father Sun gave a mighty laugh, returned the prism to the sky, and the little gray fairies turned back into the lovely colors of red, and orange, and yellow, and green, and blue, and purple – for there couldn't be a rainbow without every single one of them.

Never again did they argue about whose job was most important, because of course, every job – big or small, adds to the beauty of life in the Enchanted Forest.

The Tending of Possum Buddy

Once upon a time, in the Enchanted Forest, Keystone, the one-eared beaver, sat on a rock next to the pond. He was waiting for his good friend Possum Buddy. They would often sit together at the pond in the evening, listening to the sounds of the forest, munching on rhubarb, and watching the sun set behind Purple Mountain. He waited and waited and waited. Slowly the sun began to sink behind the mountain, but still - no Possum Buddy. Keystone watched as the sky turned from orange, to pink, to purple, and then finally there was no light left in the darkened sky. Keystone was worried.

He lumbered off to Possum Buddy's little log. He peeked into the log and saw Possum curled up into a ball. "Hey, Possum Buddy," he whispered, "I've waited all evening for you. Are you okay?"

"Oh Keystone," moaned Possum, "thank you for checking on me. I feel very bad tonight. My tummy hurts and I'm quite cold! I can't seem to get warm."

"Don't worry, little buddy. I'll take care of you," comforted Keystone. He gathered leaves and grass from around Possum's log, and gently tucked them around Possum, covering him as best as he could. Then he quickly disappeared into the dark night to find Tiger Moth, the great night messenger. By morning time, the creatures of the forest had all received the message about their good friend, Possum Buddy. Charlie Gnome was busy gathering chamomile and peppermint for a yummy, warm tea to sooth Possum's tummy. Yellow-tailed squirrel gathered wild flowers from the meadow to cheer Possum up. Boady and Bog, the toad and frog, practiced their scales in preparation to sing a healing tune to their sick friend.

By mid-morning, many creatures had gathered at Possum Buddy's log. Bog Frog and Boady Toad crooned a lovely song that lifted Possum's spirits. He listened as he sipped the lovely tea that Charlie Gnome had made him, and that Honey Bee had sweetened with delicious honey. Song birds joined in the singing, and squirrel decorated Possum Buddy's log with the bright, fragrant flowers she had gathered in the meadow. Possum Buddy's eyes grew sleepy as he finished his tea, but just before he fell asleep, Dew Drop Dawn, (who had a bushy tail, red ears, black eyes and a nose, but was *always* just whatever Dew Drop chose), crawled into his log and snuggled up next to him. She wrapped her bushy red tail around his tummy, put her arms around his neck, and whispered into his ear, "I'm a big, warm blanket." Then Possum Buddy and Dew Drop Dawn slept the morning away.

Possum Buddy woke up late that afternoon. His tummy ache was gone, and thanks to Dew Drop Dawn, (the big, thick, warming blanket), he was no longer chilled. He was feeling much better! He peeked out of his flower-covered log and saw his friends still gathered around; sitting and singing and chatting with each other - and he felt such love and gratitude for his family of forest friends, that had taken care of him and had watched over him all day!

Later that evening, he and Keystone Beaver sat next to the pond, and shared a delicious stalk of rhubarb, while they watched the sun go down behind Purple Mountain.

The Wandering Chick

Once upon a time, in a village just outside of the Enchanted Forest, there was a farm. Cows, goats, and chickens lived on this farm. A gentle farmer, named Henrietta, took care of all of the animals, treating them with great kindness. In return, the cows and goats shared their milk, and the chickens happily shared their eggs with the farmer.

One summer, a broody hen laid a clutch of eggs and hatched five, beautiful, baby chicks. The chicks followed their mother around the barnyard and learned to peck and scratch in the dirt. One little chick, however, was always curious about this-and-that, and would often wander away from his family to investigate things on the farm. One day, mama hen found him splashing around in the mud, in the pig pen. Another day, she searched high and low and finally found him curled up with the kittens in the hay in the barn. "Stay with your family!" Mama warned. "There are chicken-hawks in the sky that would swoop down on a little chick like you. The flock is the safest place for you. Roosters will warn of hawks, and we can quickly hide you from the dangers of the sky." But, the little chick desired to know more about what lay beyond the barnyard.

One afternoon, the little chick looked across the field and saw a large mulberry tree with many birds eating from its branches. "I wonder what they're eating," thought the little chick. Without another thought, he skipped and skittled all the way across the field, to where the tree stood in a valley, just outside of the Enchanted Forest. The little chick happily pecked at the purple mulberries scattered under the tree. Suddenly, the birds in the branches grew quiet and held very still. A chicken-hawk had spotted the little chick, and now soared high above the valley, watching him. "Tweet twit! Tweet twit..." sang a brave, little, brown bird, sitting very still in the mulberry tree. "Wake up, Charlie Gnome, there is danger in the valley," tweeted the bird.

A little gnome lay sleeping in the shade of the mulberry tree. He heard the little, brown bird's warning and awoke. As he opened his eyes, he saw the hawk soaring high over the valley. At first, he wasn't concerned. He loved the hawk and the hawk loved him, for Charlie Gnome was a helper to *all*. But as Charlie Gnome became fully awake, he saw the careless, little chick pecking and scratching under the tree, and Charlie Gnome immediately jumped to action! The hungry chicken-hawk swooped down from the sky, startling the little baby chick. The chick looked for a place to hide, but the hawk was too close, and now the chick was *very* frightened. Just then, the little gnome jumped onto a rock and shouted "Fly on by, dear hawk my friend, this chick is not your meal! You'll find there's food abundant in the meadow and the field." Then he covered the little chick with his body, just as the hawk swooped under the tree. The hawk, seeing the gnome's little, red hat, continued right over the chick, leaving him alone on this day, for the hawk didn't want to upset his friend Charlie Gnome.

"Get ye home now, little chick! This place is *not* for you. Run on back to mama hen. Now shoo, shoo, SHOO!" and the gnome clapped his hands very loudly. The little chick took off across the field, *tickety, tickety*, running home to the safety of his flock. There he rejoined mama hen and his siblings, as they scratched for worms in the compost bin, while the mighty barnyard rooster stood vigilantly by.

The little chick looked across the field at the mulberry tree, remembering the sweet taste of the mulberries. Maybe someday when he was a mighty rooster himself, he would return - but not today!

Water Song

𝕺nce upon a time, in the Enchanted Forest, Keystone Beaver decided to build a dam. Keystone was a one-eared beaver who was very good at dam building, but he was often very distracted by the beautiful sounds of the forest. This made it hard for him to concentrate on his important work. One morning, as he was busy gnawing on an old, dead tree that stood next to the creek, he heard Bog Frog and Boady Toad singing in unison on the bank. Their song was so lovely that he had to stop his gnawing and listen. Soon, the lovely chorus of the cousins lulled him to sleep. When he awoke, he was disappointed to see that he hadn't gotten very far in taking down the tree. He began again to gnaw at the tree with his strong, orange teeth. As he worked, he thought about how lovely his dam would be, and how happy he would be to raise his family there. Suddenly, from a cluster of pines, there came the beautiful song of the whip-poor-will. Keystone ventured over to the pines. Maybe he'd be lucky enough to see the little bird. After shuffling about the trees for some time, he realized he would never find the lovely whip-poor-will, so he headed back to his tree. The afternoon was now almost over and he had not made much progress on felling the tree.

"Oh dear, why can't I concentrate! I'll never get my dam made if I can't pay attention to my work!"

As he fretted over this problem, Charlie Gnome, who had been resting under a mayapple nearby, sat up and called to Keystone.

"Beaver friend, don't despair, the woods are full of sound. Perhaps the song you need to hear is water falling down!"

Keystone smiled and waved at Charlie Gnome. He didn't know what the gnome was talking about, but Charlie Gnome was a great helper to all animals, and he didn't want to be rude. Charlie Gnome disappeared through the woods to find his good friend, one of the rain fairies. He knew that beavers were most motivated to work on their dams when they heard the sound of running water. When he found her, he whispered in her ear, and she flew off to find the one-eared Beaver standing very close to a bush, watching a cicada rattle his love song over the forest.

The little rain fairy climbed onto a branch, high in a tree, close to where Keystone was working. She swung her little feet over the leaves and big drops of rain fell from her toes - splashing from one leaf to another, all the way down the tree, making a little puddle of water at the bottom of the tree, and turning into a tiny stream. The tiny stream bubbled and tumbled its way into the creek, making a delightful sound as it fell across the stones. Keystone turned his head. What was this he was hearing? - The lovely song of water! Suddenly, the one-eared beaver felt very excited about his dam, and scuttled back over to his tree. As he listened to the falling water, he chomped, chewed and gnawed with great energy! Finally, the tree fell, making a big splash in the creek - landing exactly where Keystone had planned. The little rain fairy shook the last droplets from her toes, and happily flew off into the night. Keystone Beaver watched her go, then he turned and looked toward the mayapples, where Charlie Gnome sat; his eyes twinkling in the dark.

"You always seem to know, don't you, dear gnome friend?" whispered Keystone Beaver, "You always seem to know."

A Lovely Stone for Dragon

𝒪nce upon a time, in the Enchanted Forest, a little girl sat on a large rock, next to a sparkling pool of water. She was waiting for her dear friend, the little, green dragon. Deep in her pocket she held a special gift she had brought for her friend. On the bank next to her, a frog and a toad skillfully mixed their songs, sending a chain of bubbling notes out across the water. The girl watched a busy, one-eared beaver across the way as he collected sticks. He stopped for a moment to listen to the lovely chorus of the frog and toad, and then hurried off to the creek with his bundle of twigs. A beautiful, yellow swallowtail landed softly on the girl's knee. She held very still as she studied the blue spots at the end of the delicate butterfly's wing. "Butterflies only land on the kind-hearted," said the little green dragon, as he sat down next to her on the rock. The butterfly flicked its wings and flew away.

"Hello, little girl,"

"Hello, dear dragon. It's been quite a while. How have you been?"

"Oh, mostly good, I guess."

"Mostly?"

"Yes, well... sometimes I do things that upset my friends, and then I don't feel so good."

The girl was silent. She watched an old groundhog and a little skunk drink together from the bank. A great blue heron landed in the water next to the them. Groundhog and the little skunk looked up, and the frog and toad suddenly became very quiet and then disappeared. The dragon continued, "You know how much I love shiny things. Sometimes I get so excited when I see sparkly, shiny, beautiful things, and then I do things that I don't mean to do. This makes my forest friends very upset." The dragon peeked over at the girl. She nodded her head - for she understood this. Then he said quietly, "I can't always do myself as I know I should." They watched as a dragonfly skipped across the water, and then the girl spoke. "Dragon, I brought you something shiny and beautiful." From her pocket she pulled out her hand and opened it. A lovely, rose quartz, in the shape of a heart, shone brightly in her palm. "From my heart to yours," she whispered. The dragon gently touched the beautiful stone. A little tear of gratitude for how the girl loved him always, trickled down his green nose and landed in the center of the heart. Just then, the great blue heron leapt gracefully from the water. The girl and dragon watched as her powerful wings lifted her into the air - her long legs trailing behind her as she disappeared across the water.

"Oh, how wonderful it would be to fly!" exclaimed the girl. "It is a wonderful thing, isn't it, little green dragon?"

"Wonderful indeed!" said the dragon, "Climb up!"

Then the little girl climbed onto the dragon's back, and the friends disappeared over the trees.

Carpenter Bee & Honey Bee

Once upon a time, in the Enchanted Forest, two little, busy bees met on a beautiful autumn day. Summer had come to a slow end, and the leaves on the trees were now red and yellow and orange and brown. Many leaves were already spread across the forest floor. Hummingbird was gone – she'd left for her long journey south. Monarch butterfly, and her friends, had also left to find warmer forests in the south. They would all return in the springtime. The squirrel with the yellow tail was busy gathering and hiding nuts, and mushrooms, and berries. Later in the winter, when the snow came, she would have yummy food to eat.

Though the forest was a bit quieter with so many birds and other creatures gone or sleeping, a tiny buzz could still be heard. Two, little, busy bees buzzed above two purple turtlehead flowers that remained in the forest. They were feasting on the nectar. "Hello," said a little bee, "I'm a honey bee"

"Hello, honey bee. I'm a carpenter bee. How is your flower?"

"Very good! How is yours?"

"Very good as well!"

They continued to gather the lovely sap, and then the honey bee said, "Carpenter bee, have you noticed that there aren't many flowers left in the forest?"

"Yes, honey bee. I have noticed that. It seems that summer is ending. Well, goodbye, honey bee. I'll see you tomorrow!"

But when the morrow came, there was only one flower left on the forest floor. "Good morning, honey bee! Can I share your flower with you?" asked carpenter bee. "Most certainly," said honey bee, "It's big enough for both of us!" So, the two little friends drank from the same flower. Then carpenter bee said, "Honey bee, what will you do when winter is finally here and there are no more flowers on the forest floor?"

"Well, my sisters and I have worked very hard all summer collecting and storing honey in our hive. When the flowers are gone, we will return to the hive and spend the winter eating the honey we have saved. We will beat our wings and make the hive nice and warm when it's cold outside. In the spring we will come back out of the hive and start collecting again! What will you do, carpenter bee?"

"Oh, I don't have a hive. I've been very busy eating as much as I possibly can lately to get nice and fat for winter. When winter finally comes, I will burrow into a nice warm log and go into a deep sleep. I will sleep all winter, and when the spring comes, I will come back out again."

"Yes! I noticed that you have a fat, little tummy!" laughed the honey bee, "Now I know why! See you tomorrow carpenter bee!"

But when the morrow came, and the carpenter bee returned to the forest, there were no flowers. Little honey bee was nowhere to be seen. A cold wind blew through the trees, scattering the leaves across the forest floor, and a little golden-crowned sparrow sang his lovely song of fall.

"Honey bee must have gone back to her hive with her sisters. I do hope that I see her again next spring."

Then the fat, little, carpenter bee gave a very big yawn, and disappeared into a hole in a log, and fell fast asleep.

The Pine on the Hill

A pine stood small, but lovely, on a hill next to a wood
Far off and to a distance, other pine trees also stood

Their branches strong and sturdy, reaching long; their trunks stood tall
But the pine upon the hill, was bent and seemed to be quite small

In the Christmas season, from the village, children came
As their parents chose the perfect tree, they'd play their little games

Of hide and seek, and run and jump, and sliding down the hill
Then one small child saw the tree, and staring, stood quite still

"Oh tree, your trunk is crooked, and you've a bald spot on one side
You look to be quite scrawny, and no good place to hide"

But something about the little pine touched her way down deep
So, she hid behind it anyway, in her game of hide and seek

Snuggled up behind the tree, she found a little hole
And when she put her eye up close, inside she saw a mole

Curled up in a little ball, its hands over its nose
Warm and happy in this spot, a perfect place to doze

And then her mum called loudly that they'd found the perfect tree
So up she jumped, and off she ran to join her family

And every year the folks would come and walk around the wood
To choose that perfect tree, and every year the pine still stood

And the little girl would visit. Every change the girl would see
A branch, a bump, a knot; another hole within the tree

And though it still stood crooked, every year it'd grow a bit
As would the girl, who now would climb up in a branch to sit

She'd marvel at its pine cones, or the nests built in the spring
That once held baby birds, now grown, and from the trees would sing

Until one year the girl didn't come. The tree watched from the hill
The children, running, jumping, playing in the snow until

Their parents called them all to come, and soon they all were gone
And the pine tree stood there silently; still bent and all alone

But year on year the pine tree grew, now taller than the rest
Too big to be a Christmas tree, but a perfect host to guests

Squirrels and birds and animals would rest in branches high
And deer would gather down below, in the shade to lie

But never did the tree forget the friendship of the girl
Who came and saw the beauty of the pine upon the hill

Then one clear, bright, winter night, as Christmas Eve drew near
A beautiful young woman with a small child did appear

And as her husband went to find a tree within the wood
The woman and her child, underneath the pine tree stood

She gently touched its branches, and caressed the tree's smooth bark
That stretched around the mighty trunk, that stood there in the dark

And the child at her side, eyes wide open with delight
Peered deep into a little hole, that by chance, was just his height

And deep within the hole, he saw a snuggly, little mouse
Curled into a tiny ball, inside its perfect house

And the tree stood tall and mighty, quite a blessing to the world
And cherished for a lifetime, in the heart of this one girl

Share the Light

Jennifer Moore is a retired teacher. She lives with her husband in Fort Wayne, Indiana on a small farm with dogs, turkeys, and chickens. She likes to garden, walk in the woods, spend time with her grandchildren and tell stories.

Her tales of the Enchanted Forest have been told either orally or through puppetry at the SkyGarden, a Waldorf-inspired playgroup, that she facilitates with her daughter.

Seasons of Chalk In the Enchanted Forest, is her second book, in this series. More stories of the Enchanted Forest can be found in her first book, *A Chalk Walk Into the Enchanted Forest.*

www.ingramcontent.com/pod-product-compliance
Lightning Source LLC
LaVergne TN
LVRC100101080526
838201LV00103B/294